Believe in the Game

Inspirational Football Stories for Young Readers of the Football Greats and Their Faith

William Harrison

Table of Contents

Introduction

A roar shakes the night sky. Just as in the days of the Roman Colosseum, the cheers of thousands echo around the stadium. They have come from far away to watch these modern gladiators battle it out for glory. The gladiators are not out to harm each other, but they fight with the same intensity to win. This is gridiron, this is war!

Just like the warriors of old, football players do put their bodies on the line. As a contact sport, American Football is one of the most extreme and fierce games where men rush at each other head-on. Every clash of arms and legs brings a gasp and a cheer from those watching the spectacle, the same as they would in Roman days. The difference is players today are doing everything they can to stay alive, grab an oval ball, and cross a line.

How It Started

It was Walter Camp who gave American Football its unique style in 1880. Being a mixture of rugby and English football, the game evolved as new rules were added, the field was shortened with added lines (making it look like a gridiron), and the number of players was reduced to only 11 (Seaver, 2022). One of Camp's ideas was to introduce the snap instead of a scrum as used in rugby, as well as the scrimmage and forward passing. And with that, the USA had its very own sport!

American football is the most popular sport in the USA. It's one of the most-watched events in the world, with 32 teams competing during the season, ending in the Super Bowl, where the best team holds up the coveted Vince Lombardi Trophy and is crowned champions.

The sport has come a long way since the beginning, with the Super Bowl being one of the most lucrative events on the calendar. There is lots of money at stake, and putting together a roster of the most skilled sportsmen is crucial. A combination of the best star kicker, a lightning-fast running back, a clever quarterback, a solid wall of a linebacker, and all the other positions, can win you the game.

Something Extra

Even though it's a team effort of 11 players, there are always those that stand out among the rest. They are crowd favorites, spectators chanting their heroes' names every time they are on the field. They run, throw, kick, and tackle like men who have supernatural strength and abilities. These players stand out because they have something extra. They create magic with the ball.

Pudge Heffelfinger was one of these players. Back when the sport was still in its early days, two rival Pittsburgh teams offered him money to play for them—that's how good he was. In the end, he accepted $500 from one of them and ended up scoring the only touchdown in the whole game (Seaver, 2022). He was worth every cent, but he was also the very first player to be paid to play—the first professional footballer in America.

Sitting in the bleachers, watching a game, there will always be names that pop up. They may have played many years ago, or they may still be on the field wearing their team's uniform, but they have become legends. These are no ordinary players! Fans can't get enough of discussing their insane moves and their incredible athleticism. These players haven't just played the game, they've set records and won victory after victory.

These are their stories. Not just about how many times they played and won. Not only about their amazing handling of the ball. These are also the stories about how they had to dig deep, overcome obstacles, and find faith in something more than themselves in order to become the superstars that they are. Some came from poor, humble backgrounds, some had physical disabilities to deal with, and others made a stand for their beliefs.

It's time to get off the stands and make your way down to the field. Hear the crowd roar as you step onto the glistening green grass. You're about to run toe-to-toe with the best of the best. Tie your cleats tight, put your shoulder pads on, and get that helmet in place. It's going to be one exciting rush as you run alongside these players who made history.

Helpful Handoffs

Every player has something unique to teach you about how they got to play in the NFL stadiums and what they had to do to realize their dreams. At the end of each story, there are a few pointers to also help you grow, overcome those obstacles, and be the best you can be. Think of them as a handoff that leads to a touchdown or a great throw that will get you much closer to the end zone!

Chapter 1:

Tom Brady (Tom Terrific)

Career Highlights

- Super Bowl champion: 7
- Super Bowl MVP: 5
- NFL Most Valuable Player: 3
- First Team All-Pro: 3
- Pro Bowl: 15
- Most quarterback wins: 251
- Most career passing touchdowns: 649

(*Tom Brady Overview*, n.d.)

Not Picked First

It was like standing on the playground during recess. The bigger kids get to pick the teams, and of course, all the stronger, faster ones get chosen first, leaving the leftovers. Reluctantly, the captains take these scrawny remainders onto their teams. No one expects anything from these out-of-shape kids. They're just there to fill a spot while the more talented ones play the game.

This was what it was like for Tom Brady! It sounds unbelievable, considering he is one of the greatest quarterbacks ever. He has won the Super Bowl seven times, has thrown 89,214 yards in the regular season and 13,400 yards in the playoffs, has 88 playoff touchdowns, and 35 career playoff wins (Deen, 2023). Those are records that other amazing players don't even come close to.

And yet, he was not the first pick!

Sporty But Slow

Growing up, Tom was a good sportsman and was very impressive in his junior year. He was talented at baseball and football and was selected to play for both. He had to make a decision and, in the end, chose football.

But he still wasn't regarded as anything special, just average. In his freshman year, he only managed to be a third-string quarterback at Michigan University. He started a few times, losing a few games and winning some. While he wasn't the fastest, he began to memorize the playbook, using his work ethic to impress the coaches.

When it finally came time for the NFL draft, despite all his hard work and good passing, Brady was not on every team's radar. He got mixed reviews from many of the scouts: "He did not have the prototypical NFL body," "He came out kinda skinny [and] they didn't think he was strong enough," and "looked slow" (Gaines, 2023). Those are not the kind of words that describe your best pick or someone who could become the greatest in his position.

Tom Brady thought he would be chosen in the first couple of rounds and even lost his cool at one point. All the hard work seemed to be for nothing as he was passed over again and again. Little did he know, but coaches from the New England Patriots had their eye on him. They were not so worried about his physical attributes and whether he only weighed 200 pounds. They had seen something in his mental abilities, the way he thought, made plays, and could lead a team.

Tom was the 199th pick in the 6th round!

But there was still a problem for him, because he wasn't the starting quarterback! For a number of games, he was forced to sit and watch Drew Bledsoe fill that position. For many players, that could be frustrating, and they might slack off or lose faith, but Tom did the opposite—he worked even harder. He began training more, put on 15 pounds, and practiced his footwork in his apartment every day.

Getting a Break

His break finally came when Drew Bledsoe suffered an injury after being flattened by his opponent, putting him out of the game for the season. Tom was finally in, but his first few games were not the best. His coach took him aside and reminded him of the way he used to play in Michigan.

Even with Bledsoe back, Tom was the Patriots starter, and he proved his worth by getting them to the Super Bowl. Against a much stronger Rams team, he led his team to victory with a stunning play in the final seven seconds to come out on top at 20–17. He was MVP ,and the Patriots suddenly ruled the NFL (Gaines, 2023). Tom's hard work had paid off. By believing in his abilities, he found a way to the top of his game.

The Patriots would go on to do it again and again, holding the trophy up seven times, thanks to Tom. It is the most times a quarterback has ever secured victory for his team at the biggest tournament, all because he worked hard and never gave up.

Living Legend

He may have been one of the slowest quarterbacks of all time, and he may have been one of the thinnest, but he was definitely one of the hardest-working players. His ability to memorize the playbook and read the other team gave him a much greater advantage over all the other faster, bigger opponents. Today, he is rated as one of the best. Some even call him the GOAT (greatest of all time).

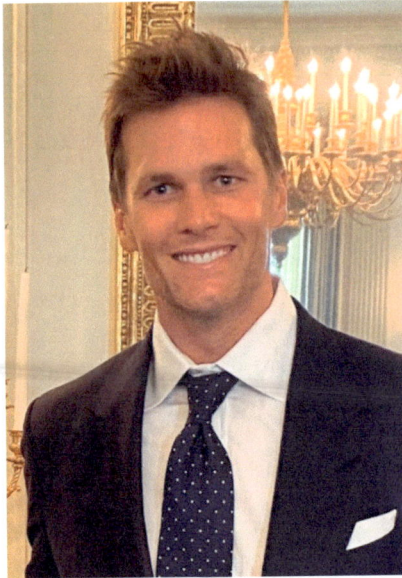

Tom Brady continues his love for the sport as he looks to step into the role of commentator. His insights into the game delight fans and players as he speaks from experience as someone who has battled it out on the gridiron, through ups and downs, to rise to greatness.

Helpful Handoffs

In the same way that Tom proved his worth as a player and a person, you can do that, too:

- **Know what makes you happy:** When you do things that bring you joy, then you are definitely in the right place, even if you're not in the top team yet.

- **Know what your personal best is:** Don't always compare yourself to others or think that winning is what it's all about. If you do the best you can do, that will get you far.

- **Work on your weaknesses:** Instead of just doing what you're good at, try becoming better at other things too. This will help you go far in many areas.

Chapter 2:

Peyton Manning (The Sheriff)

Career Highlights

- Super Bowl champion: 2
- NFL Most Valuable Player: 5
- Most passing touchdowns in a season: 55
- Most touchdown passes in a game: 7

- Super Bowl MVP: 1
- First Team All-Pro: 7
- Pro Bowl: 14

(*Peyton Manning*, n.d.)

Hard Work

There are lots of players in the NFL who are incredibly gifted at handling the ball, running, blocking, and making plays. But being excellent at something is not just about talent. Just because someone is really good at a sport does not mean they will become the best! As Tim Notke, a basketball coach, said, "Hard work beats talent when talent doesn't work" (Schoenbeck, 2023).

Peyton Manning is one of the best examples of a quarterback who had more than enough skill to command the field. But he took it an extra step further by putting in time and effort to understand, memorize, and know every single aspect of the game. This is what made him better than good.

Family Tradition

There was no surprise when Peyton went on to become a football star. He was born into a football-mad family. His father played in the NFL for 13 years, most of them for the Saints, where he had respectable stats as a quarterback. Peyton's eldest brother, Cooper, was destined to be one of the best receivers until a spinal issue stopped him from ever playing again. His youngest brother, Eli, also picked up the ball and started his own football career.

At 4 years old, Peyton could pull off a seven-step dropback and throw a Nerf ball across the living room of their house (Bradley, 1993). Watching old tapes of games with their father, all three boys learned how to analyze the defense. Sometimes, Peyton would stay and examine the footage long after his brothers had left, insisting that he needed to learn in order to become a great quarterback. Added to this, he was extremely competitive, focusing so much time on the game that his father insisted he go out and find a girlfriend!

Playing for the University of Tennessee Volunteers, he began as a third-string quarterback and struggled to make an impact. It wasn't until he was the team's starter that the passes and touchdowns fell into place. His team went on to rack up a number of back-to-back wins to end a very successful season. By the time he came to his senior year, Peyton had won all kinds of awards, including the Johnny Unitas Golden Arm Award and the Best College Player ESPY award.

The Uphill Climb

With an impressive 89 touchdowns and 11,201 yards, he had put his name on the map and was the first overall pick in the 1998 NFL Draft (Brobeck, 2016). He memorized the playbook within a week of joining the Colts. Even though their new quarterback ended up third in yards and fifth in touchdown passes, the Colts did not manage anything very spectacular that season. The following period was better, but it would be a long climb for Peyton to get to the top.

After going toe-to-toe with Tom Brady and losing to the Patriots a few times, things began to turn for Peyton's Colts. After setting a league record of 49 seasonal touchdown passes in 2004, others started to take more notice. He became known as "The Sheriff" because he laid down the law on the field, and he also commanded the utmost respect from his own teammates. They all knew that nobody researched different tactics and plays more than he did.

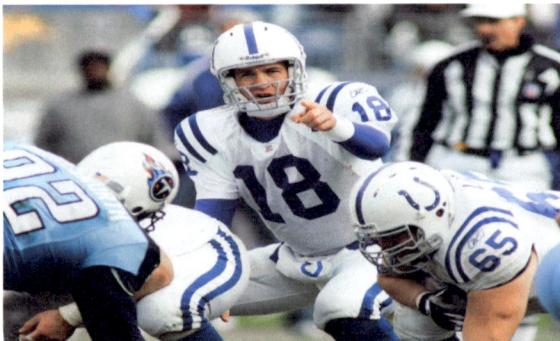

It wasn't until 2006, when he came up against Brady again, that Peyton would lead his team to a stunning comeback and beat the Patriots 38–34. This set them up to go into their first Super Bowl, where they cunningly defeated the strong Chicago Bears to win. It would be a couple of years before they would get to play in the league championship again, narrowly being denied another chance to hold up the trophy.

A neck injury would put Peyton out of the game for a while, ending his time at the Colts in 2012 with 208 consecutive starts (Brobeck, 2016). But his playing days were not over, and he led the Denver Broncos to the Super Bowl twice, winning it for them in 2015.

For somebody who was good at what he did, Peyton never slacked or rested on his talent—he put in 110%. "Every day, he was there before everyone else, and every day, he left after everyone. After practice, you'd see the man in the weight room getting stronger, and then he'd be back watching more film. Every single day" (Gagnon, 2016).

Personal Faith

It wasn't just on the field, but off it too that he gave his all. Peyton visited kids in the hospital, donating time and money through his Peyback Foundation to help those he could. He not only learned their names and things about them but also their families. It's just another example of his complete dedication and effort that has made him more than just another player on the field. His skill with the ball, as well as his memory and dedication, are his legacy.

Peyton has always been clear about what's most important in his life, and it isn't football! Although he gives everything he has when he is training or playing, he puts more focus on other things. "I rank those priorities as: faith, family, and education, then football... as important as football is to me, it can never be higher than fourth [place]" (Straeter, 2023). As a Christian and a family man, Peyton's commitment to Christ and his wife and kids comes before the game.

Helpful Handoffs

Peyton showed how hard work pays off, and you can follow his example with these tips:

- **Do the best you can:** Giving your all in every game or situation is not just about impressing others, it's about pushing to see how much you have inside you.

- **Take time out:** There is a time for pushing yourself to the limit, and then a time to reward yourself with a break. It's important to have both in balance!

- **Keep motivated:** Find ways to keep yourself going. By reading about or watching players or people you admire, you can be inspired.

Chapter 3:

Cool and Crazy Coaches

As amazing as the players on the field are, they would be like kids in a candy store without a coach. These are the guys who bring the team together, giving each person their position and working out a strategy to beat the other teams. There have been some who are like generals leading a well-oiled army into war. There are also those with some insane ideas that have been more like organizing a prom after-party than a team in the NFL!

Most Super Bowls

The Super Bowl is the climax of the football season. It is the mountaintop that all teams want to reach. Many have climbed that hill, only to fall short just before the summit by being beaten. To win the trophy is an achievement, and some have done it more than others simply because of their coach's leadership.

A number of coaches could fill the top spot, but only one of them has taken his team to the Super Bowl more than any other. While there are 32 coaches who have got their teams to the finals, only Bill Belichick has managed to win six titles. Not only that, but he did it all with the same team: The New England Patriots in Super Bowls XXXVI, XXXVIII, XXXIX, XLIX, LI, and LII. He managed to get to the championships another three times, losing out by one score each time (Rollins, 2020).

Signing Babies

Coaches have to be clever, always trying new ways to be better than their opponents. One of these is to get the freshest, hottest, best talent before anyone else. Signing the next greatest player is a surefire way to get your team to the top. That's why the draft is so important.

James Franklin, who oversaw the Vanderbilt University and Penn State teams, found a unique way to get the talent before anyone else did. He would offer scholarships to them before they're even born! "If I see a 6'6" man walking in the mall with his wife, and she's 6'2" and she's pregnant, I'll go up and offer their unborn child [a scholarship]. I'm not exaggerating. I do that all the time" (Marie, 2013). It's one way to make sure you have the best team in the future!

Eating Grass

Sometimes, a coach will go the extra mile to harness his team's energy or get them in sync. Often, it's about getting them into the right mindset, especially when they're playing at a different stadium. Getting to know the field is important if you want to have that extra edge on your opponents.

Les Miles must be a good coach. He's led LSU to a record of 85–21 and has won championships and a national title. But he also has an odd way of gaining an understanding of the ground where they are playing. He makes the players eat the grass! That's right—to know the field is to taste it! "I have a little tradition that humbles me as a man, that lets me know that I'm a part of the field and part of the game. You should have seen some games before this. I can tell you one thing: The grass in Tiger Stadium tastes best" (Marie, 2013).

Most Wins

Those people who say winning is not everything, obviously haven't played or watched American Football. Nobody wants to be on the losing side. Everyone wants to be victorious. Unfortunately, with two sides playing, there can only be one winner. The right coach can get his team to click so well that he inspires and motivates them into a winning spree.

Don Shula has two incredible records. The only perfect season in the NFL was under his watch when the Miami Dolphins ended 17–0. Not only that, but he also holds the title of coach with the most wins under his belt. When he retired, he had secured 347 wins (Marie, 2013).

Angriest Outbursts

Calm coaches are hard to find. They're just as passionate about the game as the spectators in the stands. Sometimes more so, because their job is on the line! When a touchdown is scored, the more passionate ones explode in celebration. When a penalty goes against them or something goes wrong, then it can be quite another story!

It's hard to pick the angriest, but Jim Harbaugh, who has coached the 49ers, Cardinals, and Raiders, isn't known for keeping his cool. He has kicked, screamed, thrown his clipboard onto the field in frustration, and argued with the refs on so many games that videos of his outbursts have gone viral. It's hard to keep playing when your coach is losing it on the sidelines.

Chapter 4:

Patrick Mahomes

(The Grim Reaper)

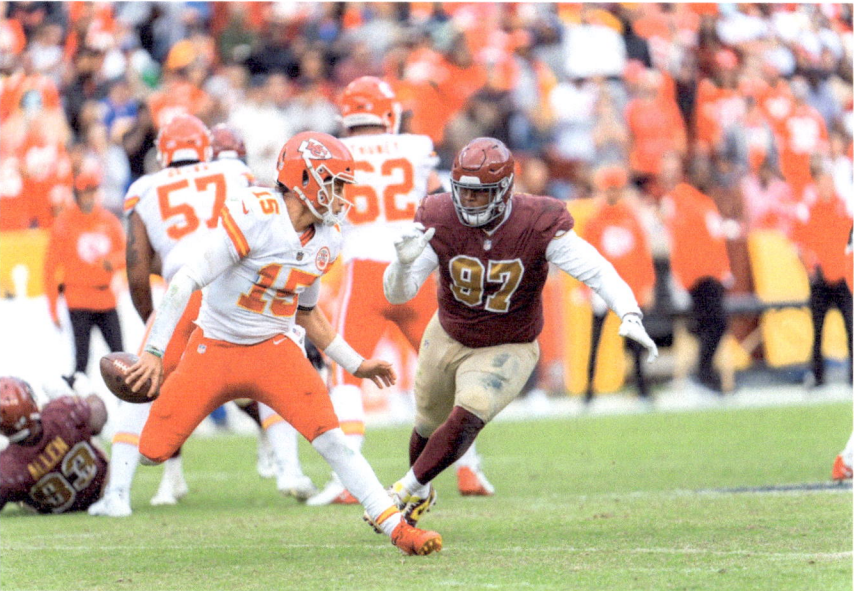

Career Highlights (So Far)

- Super Bowl champion: 2
- Super Bowl MVP: 2
- NFL Most Valuable Player: 2
- First Team All-Pro: 2
- Total yards by a quarterback in a season: 5,614
- Pro Bowl: 5
- Passing touchdowns in one postseason: 11

(*Patrick Mahomes Overview*, n.d.)

Born With Talent

Some people are just born gifted. Mozart was just a kid when he was invited to play music for the imperial courts. Judit Polgar was only 15 when she became the Grandmaster of Chess. Michael Chang won the French Open Tennis Championship at 17. There are so many who are naturally brilliant at what they do. Patrick Mahomes is one of those people.

Every time he is on the field, he lights it up with his energetic plays, his incredible arm, and his charismatic smile. One of the hottest stars of the modern game, and many people think he could go further than Tom Brady and others if he carries on the way he is. With only six seasons under his belt, he still has so much to show the world.

Many Choices

Maybe it's because his father played professional baseball, and watching his dad play around the country could definitely have rubbed off on him. Perhaps it was the fact that MLB legend Alex Rodriguez was also often around. Whatever it was, the young boy showed he had talent from a very early age.

At any game with a ball, Patrick excelled. Of course, with his father as a pitcher for the Sox, Cubs, and Rangers, baseball was his favorite sport growing up. He also loved basketball and occasionally played some football. Learning to throw and pitch, he became really good at using his arm and could get the ball to go almost exactly where he wanted it. During some of the warm-up games with his dad, he would practice by shagging (catching) the fly balls. Even then, those who were watching knew there was something special about the 5-year-old kid.

Through high school, he played both baseball and football, but many thought he would simply take up from where his father left off and be a pitcher. He was selected by the Detroit Tigers in the 2014 MLB Draft but instead chose to go to Texas Tech, where he found some success as a starter. It was here that he earned himself a name as one of the best up-and-coming quarterbacks with 11,252 passing yards, 93 touchdown passes, and 115 touchdowns that he was responsible for (Lopez, 2023).

A No-Brainer

Nicknamed "Showtime" by his dad, he did just that when it came to showing off his skills before the NFL draft. Patrick wound up his arm, sending the ball time and again straight to the receiver. To finish up, he threw a near 80-yard pass and was a top-ten pick for the Kansas City Chiefs in 2017 (Lopez, 2023).

Starting behind Alex Smith, Patrick had to wait for his time to come to show what he was really made of. In 2018, he was named MVP after equaling the record of throwing 50 touchdowns in one season, the youngest to do so.

The following year, Patrick led his team to the ultimate stage when they pulled off a Super Bowl win against the 49ers. They almost did it again in 2020, reaching the finals but just falling short of the Tampa Bay Buccaneers. Even an ankle injury could not stop this rising quarterback from glory as he overcame it to win the Chief's second Super Bowl in only four years.

His ability to bounce back was best seen when his side was down in a game against the Bills with only 13 seconds left. "When it's grim, be the Grim Reaper," his coach told him (Epstein, 2022). Changing tactics and handing a pass to go down the center of the field, he showed calm under pressure. Not only that, but he showed leadership and maturity by heading straight down and encouraging his opponents.

Choosing Faith

For a young man who is in the prime of his football career, Patrick continues to shine as one of the best quarterbacks out there. It's certainly a gift, but it's not one he boasts about or uses for his own glory. As a Christian, he is quick to turn the spotlight off himself and onto God.

Having ball skills doesn't always make you the best player. It's more than that. And Patrick Mahomes realizes there is more to sports than the ball—it's about belief. He has been clear that he doesn't just play for himself, but to glorify God, who gives him the strength to go out there onto the field. "As long as I'm doing everything the right way and the way that (God) would want me to do it, then I can walk off the field with my head held high and be able to be the man that I am" (Dallas, 2023).

Named Sportsperson of the Year in 2022 because of his active role in society, Patrick continues to make the right choices on and off the field.

Helpful Handoffs

Patrick knows what he's good at, and you can also learn to develop your skills by doing these:

- **Know your talent:** Everybody is good at something. If you're not sure what your gift is, ask others or try different things until you find it.

- **Grow your gift:** Being talented is great, but you can become even better if you work at it. Learn from others who are skilled the same way you are.

- **Don't boast:** You might be good at something, but it doesn't mean you're better than everyone else. There is always room to learn, so stay humble.

Chapter 5:

Walter Payton (Sweetness)

Career Highlights

- Super Bowl champion: 1
- Super Bowl MVP: 2
- Most consecutive starts as running back: 170

- NFL Most Valuable Player: 1
- First Team All-Pro: 5
- Pro Bowl: 9

(*Walter Payton*, n.d.)

A Good Finish

It's not how you start, it's how you finish that counts! The person who wins the race is not always the one who gets off the starting blocks first; instead, it's the person who brings it all together at the end, to push the hardest to get over the line. There are many NFL players who began their careers in football with promising futures. Scouts and critics all saw something special when they took to the field. But somewhere, they lost their way, ran out of steam, and became another side note in the game's history.

Walter Payton didn't start well. In fact, he wasn't really keen on playing football at all! When he did get into the NFL, his first season was one to forget. After he retired from football, he ran into some trouble. But when he died, the entire country mourned and remembered him for his outstanding abilities as a football star and a human being. He finished the race well!

Not the First Choice

Walter was the youngest of three kids, and when it came to sports, he wasn't as interested as his older brother Eddie was. Instead, he picked up the drums and joined the school band. In his spare time, he didn't play football like his sibling. He ran track and sang in the choir. Not quite the passionate start for one of the best running backs of all time.

When Eddie graduated, the coach asked Walter if he would try out. The reply was yes on one condition—he could continue playing in the school band as well. In his very first game, Walter charged 65 yards to score. If that wasn't enough, he followed it up with a 75-yard sprint to the touchdown line.

Walter was not only fast, but he was quick on his feet, able to dodge and weave, leaving the opposite defense in confusion. His senior year was 1970, and it was not easy as Black schools like his were integrating with White ones. What could have been a racially tense explosion, turned out to be a winning formula as Walter and his teammates merged to bring victory.

Walter scored in every single game of his junior and senior years. He went on to join Jackson State University, where his brother, Eddie, had been. As a running back, Walter set the conference alight with 651 yards and five touchdowns in 1971, and then 781 yards and 15 touchdowns in 1972 (Donahue, 2022). Records were broken as he scored seven touchdowns and two, two-point conversions in one game against Lane College and 279 rushing yards! It was no surprise that he was named Black College Player of the Year more than once while he was at Jackson State.

This was when he got his nickname, "Sweetness." Some say it was because of the great person he was, but another story adds a different version. When Walter easily dodged a tackle in practice, he yelled over his shoulder, "Your sweetness is your weakness!" (Donahue, 2022).

A Rocky Start

1975 saw the Chicago Bears snatching up Walter Payton to be part of their team. They had seen his impressive skills and the records he had set in his four years at Jackson State. But they wouldn't be overly impressed with the signing, as the new running back scored no points off eight carries in his first game. Walter took time to adjust and ended the season with relatively good stats.

He went on to improve on those scores in 1976, cementing his role at the Bears. The following year, he came off with 339 carries for 1,852 yards (his best), 14 touchdowns, and set an NFL record when he rushed 275 yards in a single game against Minnesota, even though he was recovering from flu (Donahue, 2022). In 1979, the Bears made the playoffs.

Over the next few years, the team would go through some changes and struggle to find their winning formula even though Sweetness continued to dominate in his position. It wasn't until 1985 that things began to click again, and the Bears charged through the season and into the Super Bowl XX against the Patriots. There, they romped to a 46–10 victory without Walter scoring a single touchdown (Donahue, 2022)!

He retired a few years later, having picked up many awards and trophies on the way: a Super Bowl champion, nine-time Pro Bowler, five-time first-team All-Pro, a league rushing yards, attempts and scoring leader, NFL MVP and Offensive Player of the Year, Man of the Year, and Bert Bell Award winner (1985) (Donahue, 2022).

Ending Strong

Walter Payton could never sit still and always had a joke to tell. After his NFL career, he tried a number of things, but nothing quite worked out. And then he got a rare liver disease. He lost weight and soon wasn't able to move from his bedroom. It was not the way an all-star running back should end up. But Walter knew that there was more to life than awards, accolades, and records.

He asked his former teammate, Mike Singletary, to be with him in those last days, to sit by his bed and read from the Bible. Every day until Walter died, the two men read and prayed. It might seem like a bit of a soft, sad ending to such a brilliant career, but there's more to life than winning every game and getting to the Super Bowl. Walter realized this, and he wanted to finish off with his faith strong.

Walter put it best when he said, "Never die easy. Why run out of bounds and die easy? Make that linebacker pay. It carries into all facets of your life. It's okay to lose, to die, but don't die without trying, without giving it your best" (admin, 2022).

Many colleagues didn't just remember the way he played, but also the kind of man he was. He would knock you down hard in a tackle but then stick around to help you back up afterward. He had a big heart. Because of his character on and off the field, the trophy for the best player of each season was renamed The Walter Payton NFL Man of the Year award.

Helpful Handoffs

You can also learn from Walter how to stay true all the way by putting these into action:

- **Stay on track:** Keep checking your goal or dream to make sure you are going in the direction you wanted to in the first place.

- **Be accountable:** Find someone who can keep encouraging you to go the distance. Everybody needs some motivation, and other people can help by reminding you to keep going.

- **A very long-term goal:** It's not just about sports, music, business, or money. Start thinking about the kind of person you want to be when you grow up. Aim for that!

Chapter 6:

Bad Breaks

Football is a contact sport! Injuries are bound to happen, even though every precaution is taken through rules and protective gear. Sometimes, it's a mild concussion or a few bruises. But the worst can happen when it's a bone-shattering accident that can end a career before it starts. However, the spirit of the player can often be so great that he overcomes his injury to get back on the field and keep on playing!

Alex Smith

During a 2018 game between the Houston Texans and the Rams, Alex suffered a broken leg. As quarterback, he had dropped back where his offensive line somehow let the Texans through. Alex was sacked hard for a loss of 13 yards. But it was another player that also landed on him that really did the damage. A broken fibula and tibia meant screws being inserted to fix the breaks, which later caused infections. After skin grafts and lots of rehab, Alex stepped back out onto the field again in 2020. He played eight games, starting in six to finish the season, earning him the NFL Comeback Player of the Year (Robinson, 2023).

Thomas Davis

Injured knees (ACL tears) are very common in the NFL. They can put a player out for half a season or more. Thomas Davis of the Panthers suffered three in his right knee over three seasons! But that wasn't his most courageous comeback. During a game against the Cardinals in the NFC, his arm was broken. The next day, he went through surgery, and a cast was put on. The problem for the big offensive tackler was that the team was booked for the Super Bowl two weeks later. Not one to sit out one of the biggest opportunities of his life, Thomas was on the field that day in 2015. He made seven tackles, with his arm strapped up!

Rocky Bleier

He may not have received the injuries on the field of play, but coming back from the field of battle with life-threatening wounds is worthy of respect. Rocky was in his rookie season for the Steelers when he got called up to go to Vietnam in 1968. On a day out with his troop, a bullet penetrated his left leg, and a grenade explosion filled his right one with deadly shrapnel. Doctors were thinking of amputating—it was that serious. But he returned in 1971 to continue playing for his team, going with them four times to the Super Bowl.

Peyton Manning

He had suffered neck injuries for a while and decided to have surgery—four in total. He missed an entire season and never had the same strength in his throwing arm after that. But that didn't matter. He would go on to set a stunning 55-touchdown pass record, which saw his team, the Broncos, make the Super Bowl and win (Robinson, 2023). He would also pick up two more first-team All-Pro honors, making a total of seven. Not bad for a quarterback who was not as good as he used to be!

Kendall Simmons

Not all injuries happen on the field. Some are just freak accidents. In 2006, Pittsburgh Steelers player Kendall Simmons had to miss a game due to falling asleep "chilling" while watching football on the TV. The problem was he forgot he had an ice pack on, and he ended up with a frostbite-like burn on his left foot. Fortunately, he was back in the next game.

Turk Edwards

A 1940 game had an injury before the game started! New York Giants player Turk Edwards had bad knees to start with because of all the crouching he endured in his position. So, once the coin toss had been done, he turned a little too quickly to leave the field. His cleats stuck in the grass while the rest of his body swiveled around. It was the end of his knee and the end of his career! (Passalacqua, 2011).

Chapter 7:

Jalen Hurts

Career Highlights (So Far)

- Second Team All-Pro: 1
- Bert Bell Award: 2022
- Rushing touchdowns: 33

- Pro Bowl: 1
- Sugar Bowl MVP: 1
-

(*Jalen Hurts*, n.d.)

Having a Goal

Having a goal is important. It's no good being talented and hoping that you'll make it one day. You have to direct that skill somewhere. Think big, think of your future, and head toward that. That's what makes some of the best sportsmen in the world great. They had dreams and turned them into reality.

Jalen Hurts is still just beginning his NFL career, but he is already making waves. It didn't just start when he was drafted—it began a long time back when he decided he was going to beat everyone else out for the position he wanted. It might sound arrogant and a little cocky, but his quiet confidence is what has made him one of the rising stars of the modern game.

Knowing What You Want

Jalen was born in 1998 in Texas and went to Channelview High School, where he scored 51 touchdowns. His father, the coach, helped him work on his technique and encouraged him in his powerlifting, where Jalen would push 500 pounds at a time and even make it to the regional finals. But his father also taught him two other lessons: resilience and the attitude of never staying down when you're knocked over and setting your sights higher and going for it.

With his talent with the ball, it was a disappointment when he received no scholarship from the University of Texas. Undeterred, he enrolled in the University of Alabama, where he wormed his way into the quarterback role.

He was not the starter, with other quarterbacks already in place, but he turned and said, "I'm gonna make every one of them transfer" (Conn, 2023). Through sheer hard work and a positive mindset, he did just that. All three of the older players had to make way for the new phenomenon. Posting an impressive 2,780 yards through the air and 954 on the ground in his first season, he led his team to the championships, where they were narrowly beaten (Alonso, 2023).

But he wasn't the only one who could throw, and he was benched halfway through the next national championship as his team suffered. It was a bitter lesson to have to learn. He sat on the sidelines and watched his replacement win the game. He would remain the backup for the rest of the season, no matter how hard he tried.

Living the Dream

The coaches at the Eagles were not put off by this and signed Jalen in 2020 as the 53rd pick, a move many thought was wrong. Fans and critics thought the new rookie's style was not a good match for their team, but they would soon see what the coaches had in mind. After spending time as a backup, he finally pushed his way to the front and became the starter. In his first game, he threw a touchdown pass and rushed for more than 100 yards, the first for a quarterback in his NFL debut (Munez, 2023). He led his team to victory after victory until being controversially benched in the last game.

The year 2022 saw Jalen pass for 22 touchdowns and rush for 13, showing just why the Eagles had faith in signing him. In the same season, he took the Eagles into the Super Bowl, where they fought hard, losing to the Chiefs 38–35 in the final seconds. His name would be one of the finalists for MVP of the year, as well as a Pro Bowl appearance (Munez, 2023).

The world of sports is wide open for someone who dreams big and sees far into the future, like Jalen. He signed a five-year contract with the Eagles for a whopping $255 million, which was the highest for any NFL player at the time (Munez, 2023).

Faith to Go Far

Jalen's confidence is not something that just happened—it's something he learned watching his father coach football. He saw how his father inspired, worked with players, and developed relationships. He also found his father's faith made him able to hold his head up high no matter what happened. Having a solid anchor helps Jalen steer through every storm and still find his way. That is why he says:

> It means in the midst of any situation, in the midst of whatever it is. Whatever it is you're going through, never lose your trust in God and never lose your faith in God. Keep your head down, be graceful, keep on controlling what you can. Give it to the Lord and do your best. Regardless of the situation, you may not know, now but later you'll understand. (*Faith on the Field*, 2021, para. 7)

Jalen's faith holds him steady even when he's benched. He knows that there will be disappointments and frustrations, but he also believes that God will guide him through to a new day and another chance.

Helpful Handoffs

Jalen had his goal very clear in his mind. To help you realize your goals, you can follow these steps:

- **Write down your goals:** Only having your dreams in your head doesn't make them a reality. Writing them down is important to setting goals (even if they seem too huge to achieve). Talk about them with your parents or coach.

- **Celebrate the small wins:** There will be lots of victories on the way, and it's important to see them as stepping stones to greater success. Take time to enjoy them.

- **Be ready for setbacks:** You will fail. It's part of life to make mistakes or lose sometimes. Don't see these moments as the end of your dreams but learning moments toward achieving them.

Chapter 8:

Kurt Warner (Chachi)

Career Highlights

- Super Bowl champion: 1
- NFL Most Valuable Player: 2
- Pro Bowl: 4

- Super Bowl MVP: 1
- First Team All-Pro: 2
-

(*Kurt Warner*, n.d.)

Getting Back Up

Sometimes, life can be hard and smack you down. It could be a death, an illness, or some tragedy that leaves you winded on your back. Getting hit is also part of football. A hard tackle can put a player on the grass, knocking the breath out of them. That crunch of shoulder pads clashing and bodies collapsing is all part of the game. But the test is if they get back up again, ready to play. The test is getting back up to face life when it deals you bad cards.

Kurt Warner's story is one of not being picked at all. He never got his break like all the other great players and was overlooked and undrafted. But he never gave up and fought for his place. Even that wasn't enough, as he got benched or dropped by his team, only to have to work his way back into the game where much younger, faster players were being considered over him. Kurt's faith kept him persevering through every dip so that he rose again and again.

Overlooked

Kurt was stocking shelves to make ends meet. That was it— no glamorous offer from teams, no golden ticket to the big time. He entered the 1994 draft hoping to get picked but got nothing, so he signed with the Green Bay Packers for tryouts. With Brett Favre there, he didn't really get a chance and ended up not getting a position. That led him to the local Hy-Vee Supermarket to try to make some money as a packer.

Kurt didn't let it get to him. He kept training and working until the Iowa Barnstormers of the AFL signed him in 1995, where he led them to two Arena Bowl berths (Morales, 2009). Three years later, he ended up in Amsterdam playing for NFL Europe until the St. Louis Rams brought him on as a 27-year-old rookie.

He finally got a crack at playing when the quarterback was injured. Kurt managed an impressive 4,353 passing yards and a league-leading 41 touchdowns, with the offense pulling 526 points. The team ended 13–3, and Kurt was named MVP (Hunt, 2023). It didn't stop there as the Rams flew through the playoffs and claimed the Super Bowl, with Kurt throwing the winning touchdown in the last two minutes.

After breaking his hand and missing a few games, Kurt was back in the fold, throwing to get his team a second chance at lifting the Super Bowl trophy. But going up against Brady and the Patriots was always going to be hard, and they lost. Even so, the Rams put up such a great offense over the three years led by Kurt Warner, that it was named the Greatest Show on Turf (Hunt, 2023).

Benched

Another injury saw Kurt being sidelined until he was no longer a part of the team. The New York Giants took him on as a bridge quarterback to get Eli Manning ready for the season. Without feeling threatened, Kurt showed him the ropes until he was no longer needed. Manning went on to win two Super Bowls.

Kurt's next stop was the Arizona Cardinals, where he was meant to mentor another quarterback as he did for Manning. An injury to another player saw him named starter, and he pushed hard to get his team to the playoffs, throwing 4,583 yards and 30 touchdowns (Hunt, 2023). Everything seemed right for the Super Bowl as the Cardinals were peaking at the right time, and Kurt had just been named the Walter Payton Player of the Year, but victory was stolen from them in the dying seconds of the game by a Steelers' tip-toe catch.

The following year, Kurt took the Cardinals back to the playoffs to face his old team, the Packers. This time, he went 29 of 33 passing for 379 yards and five touchdowns in a 51–

54 overtime victory that is still called one of the best playoffs by a quarterback in the NFL (Hunt, 2023). He retired soon after that and later was inducted into the Hall of Fame.

Faith

One of the reasons Kurt never gave up and continued believing was because of his strong faith and values. As a Christian, he realized it was not just something to do on Sundays but something that guided every decision, every move, and every game. A story like Kurt's is a rags-to-riches Cinderella story that might seem as if luck was on his side. But for him and his family, there was more to the breaks and chances he got. It was all part of God's plan for his life, and he gives full credit to that:

> I think that I always felt faith was kind of, well, God was out there, and whenever I needed Him, He was like my spare tire – that when I get a flat, I'll go and pop the trunk and pull out the spare and God, You know, I need this... I had this mixed up. ... I'm here to give my life for Him as Jesus did for me. And it started to become real. I started to understand and take a different perspective on what life was all about. (Foust, 2021, para. 5, 6)

Helpful Handoffs

Kurt is a great example of pushing through when things look like they may not be working out, and you can learn a few tips from him:

- **Stay true to yourself:** Changing who you are to get noticed doesn't always end well. Be who you are—genuine, authentic, and real.

- **Stick to your goals:** Even when you don't make the cut, it's important not to give up, but believe you can still get there.

- **Self-compassion:** It's good to be confident, but it is more important to see yourself as a friend—be your own cheerleader rather than criticizing yourself all the time.

Chapter 9:

Stunning and Strange Stadiums

The game of football needs a field, and it needs somewhere for the people who come and watch the game to sit, which is why the NFL has some incredible arenas for the sport. But stadiums are not just seats around a patch of grass. They are the homes of the teams. Playing on their own field means the fans will outnumber the opponents and come in droves to watch, all in the right colors. It also means the players have a good idea of the conditions of the field because it's where they practice. A great stadium is an added advantage. But not all of them are great!

Oakland Coliseum

The idea was to be able to accommodate two sports. This meant that during the off-season, other fans could come and watch a different sport, and the seats would be filled up. The problem was, a baseball field is not the same as a gridiron! Built over a diamond-shaped green, the football field stretched over dirt patches where the bases would normally be. Plus, the shape meant fans were seated far from the NFL action. If that wasn't enough, it leaked and was home to possums.

U.S. Bank Stadium

A poll of the best sports writers showed that the majority agree: This is the best stadium in America. Being an indoor field means games can be played regardless of the weather, and fans are guaranteed their money's worth. The architects were clever enough to allow enough natural light in through the glass structure to make it feel as though the game is outdoors. Costing around $1 billion, it's truly a work of art, and every game has that Vikings' atmosphere with skol war cries and fake snow (Machota, 2023).

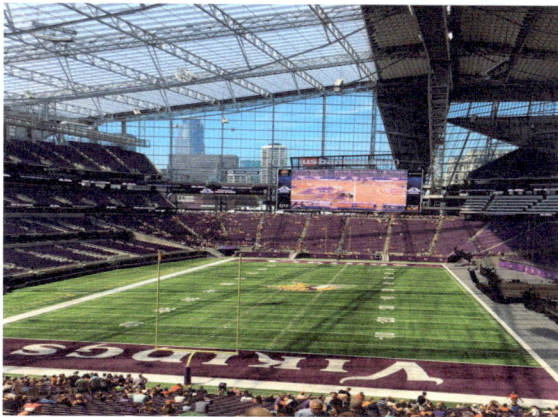

FedEx Field

Unanimously voted the worst. With more dirt than grass, this stadium has been falling apart for years. Home to the Washington Commanders team, the plumbing leaks, the railings are loose, and even though it can seat a whopping 91,000, it's an accident waiting to happen. The tickets are more costly than at other grounds, and the traffic is a nightmare, making it difficult to find decent parking that won't be a rip-off. But there are plans to upgrade, and like the teams they host, next season may be a winner (Machota, 2023).

Lambeau Field

Home to the Cheesehead Green Bay Packers, this is one of the most respected stadiums in the NFL. Opened in 1957, it can house over 81,000 spectators. Even though it's not in a major city, the drive there is worth it to witness the green and gold of the faithful fans, and maybe a famous Lambeau Leap. It can get cold and has often snowed on the pitch, but come rain or sleet, the NFL is playing.

Lumen Field

Seattle fans are known to be the loudest. But it's not just their voices—it's a combination of clever architecture and atmosphere. Built to ensure the spectators feel closer to the game than in any other stadium, as well as the echoing roof structure, a decibel reading put it close to the level of a jet engine! Fans rate this as one of their favorite grounds because they get to be a part of the action.

Soldier Field

This arena is the oldest of all the existing ones. Opening in 1924, it could house up to 74,280 spectators, but it wasn't actually used for pro football until the Chicago Bears moved in and made it their home in 1970. Changes were made to accommodate this. In 2003, more renovations were done to upgrade the infrastructure and downscale the seating capacity to 61,000. It was important in the design to try to keep the historical feel while bringing it into the modern era of sports.

Chapter 10:

Tom Dempsey (The Bomb)

Career Highlights

- First Team All-Pro: 1
- George Halas Award: 1
- Pro Bowl: 1
- Longest kick: 63 yards

(*Tom Dempsey*, n.d.)

Overcoming Setbacks

There are always problems or obstacles that can get in the way of realizing your dreams. It just happens. It might not be anything you've done or your fault, but life can throw curveballs when you least expect it. Those who find solutions and overcome these hurdles are the ones who succeed. They are the ones who believe they can do it, no matter what. That's a special kind of faith.

Tom Dempsey should not have been a football player. He was born without some of the necessary parts of the body that make an athlete really great. He could easily have given up his dream of getting out onto the field, but he didn't. Instead, he found a way to become one of the best kickers in American Football despite having no toes!

No Excuses

Born in 1947, Tom came into the world with no toes on his right foot and no fingers on his right hand. Those are quite important to have when you want to play a sport that involves kicking, running, throwing, and passing. But Tom was not deterred. His father encouraged him to follow his dreams. When young Tom was struggling with something and wanted to give up, his dad said, "Boy, you never say can't. You may have to do something differently, but you can do it" (Donahue, 2023).

At San Dieguito High School and Palomar College in San Diego, he played football, joined the wrestling team, and became a really good shot put thrower (Morthier, 2022). But his favorite was football, and he proved to be better than most, outrunning some of the other players, even without toes on his one foot.

Using his wrestling skills, he played lineman and defensive tackle. He was tough and never backed down, good enough to be chosen as an all-conference player. The team already had a kicker, but couldn't get the kick-offs right, so the coach asked if anyone could kick. Tom took off his shoe and slotted the ball out of the end zone. No one believed it, so he did it again.

Setting Records

The San Diego Chargers took him on as a free agent where they had a special boot made for him with a 2-inch block at the toe end. It looked more like a leather sledgehammer, but it did the job. In 1968, he joined the New Orleans Saints and had an average scoring rate with his kicks.

In a tense game against the Lions, there was only one point difference at 17–16 with 11 seconds left on the clock. The quarterback found the receiver, who quickly stepped out of bounds with two seconds remaining. It was time for "Stumpy," as some of his teammates called Tom because of his short boot.

The problem was that the Saints were on the Lions' 45-yard line. That meant he would have to pull off one of the longest kicks to date. Up to that point, the furthest was 56 yards. Remembering his record 63-yard kick, Tom said (Donahue, 2023):

> I was more concerned about kicking it straight because I felt like I could handle the distance. I knew I was going to get a perfect snap from Jackie Burkett and a perfect hold from Joe Scarpati. It was all up to me. I hit it sweet. (para. 33)

Some people argued that he had an advantage because of his square shoe, but Tom just laughed and told them to try and kick the same distance with only two seconds to spare!

Tom later joined the Philadelphia Eagles and kicked another 54-yard kick. His other kicking might not have been as accurate as he would have liked, with only a 60% success rate, but every so often, he got them perfectly. In 1972 and 1973, he improved by winning a game purely on kicks against the Houston Oilers and connecting on all his extra points (Donahue, 2023). His best year was in 1975, playing for the Rams when he got 83% of his kicks right.

While some critics called him a one-kick wonder, Tom proved he was not just a kicker when he made six unassisted tackles in 1974, one of them knocking the Giants' return man out cold before he got to the end zone.

Tom played for a few more teams before retiring after 11 years in the NFL. His 63-yard record kick remained unbroken until 2013.

Positive Thinking

It wasn't just in football that Tom looked on the bright side of things. Even when Hurricane Katrina flooded their home in 2005, he remained positive and said:

> I told my wife there was good news and bad news. She asked me for the good news and I told her she was

getting the new furniture she wanted a lot sooner than she thought. The bad news was that we didn't have a house to put it in. (Donahue, 2023, para. 61)

Tom Dempsey may not have been the GOAT. He may not have been the best kicker. But his belief in turning things around for good, and overcoming hardships makes him one of the all-time football heroes.

Helpful Handoffs

If you come up against setbacks like Tom did, you can try a few things to help you overcome them in your life:

- **See things differently:** Solutions come when you can look at something from different angles. What's good, bad, strange, or funny about what happened?

- **Don't blame:** It's easy to think that the reason something happened is because of someone or something. But there are many times when it's best to just accept it and move on.

- **Learn to laugh:** See the funny side of things. It really helps to not let problems get you down.

Chapter 11:

Reggie White

(Minister of Defense)

Career Highlights

- Super Bowl champion: 1
- NFL Defensive Player of the Year: 2
- Consecutive seasons with over 10 sacks: 9

- First Team All-Pro: 8
- Pro Bowl: 13

(*Reggie White*, n.d.)

More Than Football

For many Americans, football is a religion! They breathe, eat, and sleep the sport. Players are so exalted that they are worshiped. Games are more important than work or family. And the local stadium is hallowed ground! When their team wins, they are ecstatic, but when it's a loss, their world collapses around them.

While it's great to get involved, follow the players, and enjoy the game, taking it to this extreme can be unhealthy. Even those on the field know this, which is why they look for something else to ground them, to keep them centered. Some, like Reggie White, profess their faith in God and hold onto their beliefs as a foundation for their entire life, not just sports.

Two Passions

Reggie White was a big boy. Born in Tennessee in 1961, he was often teased by other kids for being larger than them. He never retaliated, but instead, he found something that fit his size: football. When he was 12 years old, Reggie told his mother that there were two things he wanted to be when he grew up: a football player and a church minister.

He stuck to his plan and went on to realize both his dreams.

In high school, he made an impact, both on the field and against other players who he flattened in tackles. In his time playing for the Hustlin' Tigers at Howard High School, he made 140 tackles, 88 of which were unassisted (Marinelli, 2022). The world opened up to him, and many universities crowded in to grab him as one of their own, but Reggie stayed close to home.

At the University of Tennessee, he continued to make a name for himself as a solid blocker, a tough tackler, and a defensive star. During his time there, the number of tackles peaked at 293, with 201 all of his own doing. At the same time, he was ordained as a minister, but this part of his life plan would have to be put on hold as his football career took off. Instead of jumping to the NFL, Reggie joined the Showboats as part of the USFL.

Solid as a Wall

After two seasons of being part of that team, the USFL folded, and the Philadelphia Eagles took him on. He wasn't well-known in the NFL, but he very quickly showed who he was as he put opponents on their backs again and again. Over the next three years, Reggie dominated the rankings in terms of sacking quarterbacks and was named Defensive Player of the Year in 1987. But while the defense was strong, the Eagles struggled to advance in terms of games.

Players knew who Reggie White was, and many feared him when he took the field.

After 1992, Reggie became a free agent and moved to the Green Bay Packers. They were a team that wasn't really worth considering, but his phenomenal contribution as a tackler put them on the map. By 1996, the team had forged their way into the Super Bowl XXXI, finally taking home the cup after exploding in the second quarter against the Patriots (Bearn, 2007). Reggie sacked Bledsoe, the opposite quarterback, three times in that game.

The Packers would visit the Super Bowl the following year and lose out in a nail-biter against the Broncos. The following year, instead of retiring like most players his age, Reggie put in another sterling effort for the Packers before moving over to the Carolina Panthers in 2000 and retiring a year later.

At the end of his 15 years in football, Reggie tallied 1,111 tackles, 198 sacks, 3 interceptions, 33 forced fumbles, and 20 fumble recoveries, with two for touchdowns (Bearn, 2007). He made the "hump move" famous, using it many times against elusive quarterbacks. He was known as a fierce brick wall when he was playing, but a gentle giant and gentleman off the field.

All for God

Although Reggie couldn't practice full-time as a minister while he was playing football, he never stopped being active in his faith. It is what shaped him as a person. He would often be seen praying before, during, and after games, sometimes with players from the opposing teams. Standing on street corners, Reggie would preach from his Bible, trying to convince young Black people that they didn't just need faith, but they had to put it into action.

As part of the Fellowship of Christian Athletes, he reached out, using his influence as a football player to share the gospel of Jesus. Together with his wife, he built a shelter for unwed mothers to stay in and get their lives back together. Always giving of himself and his money, Reggie's life was not just football—it was his belief that made him stand as tall as a giant.

Helpful Handoffs

Just like Reggie, it's good to have a solid foundation. Having a strong faith like he did will help. Here are three ways to do that:

- **Believe:** Having faith in someone or something bigger than this world is important to help you get through the bumps and obstacles of life.

- **Trust:** Learning to trust people is not easy, but it pays off when you find the right ones who will always have your back.

- **Be humble:** No one is perfect. It's important to remember that no one is better than anyone else in every way.

Chapter 12:

Rare and Ridiculous Rules

Having started over a hundred years ago, the game of football evolved as it grew. First, it was a mixture of rugby and soccer until Walter Camp defined it better. Then, as teams were added, more rules were needed to make it streamlined. While the modern game has changed a lot from what it was long ago, there are still some rules that you will find that have not gone away.

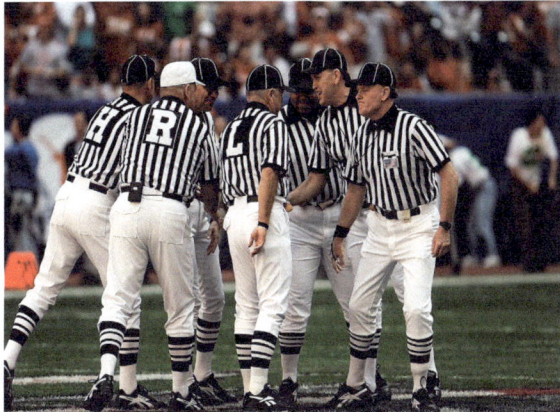

Drop Kick

The quarterback can drop the ball and kick it as it bounces on the ground. If it goes through the goalposts, it's an extra point. This comes from the game of rugby, which uses this sneaky tactic to put a quick score on the board. But in American Football, it has hardly been used. There have been a few attempts, but the only successful one was back in 1941 by Doug Flutie (Barrera, 2019).

Coin Toss Loss

Most games, like cricket, soccer, and football, have a coin toss to decide which team starts where and who has the advantage of beginning the game. Both captains go out onto the field with the referee, and a call of heads or tails will determine what happens next. But if one team fails to be at the toss with less or more than six of their players in uniform, they automatically lose the choice, and it goes to the opposing team.

Fair Catch Kick

When the receiver calls for a fair catch after a punt or kickoff, he has the option to do a fair catch kick. This means he can try and kick the ball through the posts as a free kick or drop kick. It was attempted by the 49ers in 2013 and did not work. The last successful one was back in 1976. It is a rule that is hardly ever used.

Fielding Out-Of-Bounds Kick

When a kickoff goes out of bounds without anyone touching it, the receiving team pulls to the 40-yard line. That's normal. But if a player steps out of bounds and touches the ball that's been kicked while it's still live on the field, it's called out-of-bounds. This turns a great kick into a terrible one, losing territory for the kicking team. Ty Montgomery managed to do this in 2016, and it took a while for everyone to figure out what had happened before carrying on with the game.

Snap Through the Quarterback's Legs

If a quarterback doesn't catch the ball when a center snaps it to him, and it rolls through his legs, no one else can touch the ball! Only the quarterback can do so, and if anyone else does, it becomes a false start by the offense.

Getting the Ball After a Touchdown

Usually, after a touchdown, it's simple. The team who did not score gets the ball. But the rules state that they can decide on who gets the ball. That's right. They can give it back to the opposition and make them restart if they want. That seems like giving away possession, so it's a rule no one really considers, but it's in the book!

An Unfair Act

Here's a rule that's never been used. If the referees decide that there was an illegal action that prevented a touchdown (like a benched player tackling a runner), the touchdown will be awarded. Rugby has a similar rule that it uses all the time: When a player illegally stops a try, it is awarded. But the NFL has never seen this one yet.

No Crowd Footballs

The ball often skews off a foot and lands up in the bleachers, where the crowd reaches out to make a catch. It's an exciting moment where spectators become part of the game. But as much as they would like to take it home as a souvenir, the rule is that the ball has to be returned back to the field. Fans can't keep it. Too many fights have broken out over who caught it and who kept it, and a rule was made to stop all that. That applies to players, too, as they are not allowed to randomly kick or throw a ball into the crowd. They will be fined $7,210 the first time, and $12,360 the next. They must put it in another player's hands (Freedman, 2023)!

Neat and Tidy

There are so many rules to how a player must wear their uniform on the field: Shirts must be tucked in, pants have to cover the knees, no designs on shoes in a match, towels can only be tucked into pants in the front, no bandanas, and no messages on their bodies or shirts anywhere (Freedman, 2023). There are fines if they don't get it right.

Chapter 13:

Justin Jefferson (El Jefe)

Career Highlights (So Far)

- NFL Offensive Player of the Year: 1
- Most receiving yards per game: 98.1

- First Team All-Pro: 1
- Pro Bowl: 3

(*Justin Jefferson Overview*, n.d.)

Finding the Right Fit

Everybody is talented. Each person has something that they are really good at. Often, it's very obvious. A kid effortlessly strings together music from his mind or shoots hoops without missing one after the next. Other times, it's not so evident, and it takes someone else with a keen eye to be able to see the hidden talent. They can steer, nurture, and grow it into something awesome for the whole world to see.

Justin Jefferson was a zero-star recruit who had some talent but was relatively unknown and was playing in the wrong position. It would take one coach to see what none of the other trainers could see. This man would ensure Justin went from average to awesome and achieved his potential.

Brotherly Support

Not far from the house in Saint Jose, Louisiana, where Justin grew up, there was a vacant plot, an empty stretch of grass good for nothing other than serving as a makeshift training ground. The three Jefferson boys would practice running and catching, especially for older brother, Jordan, who played for Louisiana State University as a quarterback. When they weren't kicking and passing, they would play basketball for points to increase their competitive edge.

Even though Justin credits the coaches who have been instrumental in pointing him in the right direction and showing him what to work on in order to get where he is, he pays a lot of respect to his brothers. Both Jordan and Rickey have always had his back, supporting him throughout his career.

One-on-one film sessions and extra work in the empty lot were how Jordan put his younger brother on the right path to becoming a football star. Not only that, but he had to help Justin focus so that his grades in school did not slip. Looking back, Jordan says:

> We were able to see a side of him. Maybe the country didn't see it, so it was just a matter of time before everyone else could understand his level of talent. I was able to give him two years' worth of training, worth of knowledge, and information about football defenses (Cronin, 2020, para. 12).

Justin, of course, sees how much they have helped him, and he continues to rely on their support and advice. "I lean on them with everything," he says (Mizutani, 2020).

The Right Direction

When Justin followed his older brothers to LSU, many were keen to see what he could offer. It was Steve Robicheaux who noticed the potential and hard work and began to mold Justin from a backyard nobody into a football somebody. One of the first things he did was move him from quarterback (a position Jordan Jefferson had played) to receiver. Justin clicked in this position and never looked back.

In 2019, he had an outstanding record of 111 catches for 1,540 yards and 18 touchdowns (Mizutani, 2020). Another insight into Justin's abilities came when wearables (GPS tracker and sensor) were used to study how players visually tracked a ball and which route they were most efficient in. This breakthrough technology allowed coaches to see that "Jefferson is a bilateral route runner, meaning he can run basically any route you want. He'll be able to pick it up" (Cronin, 2020).

To everyone else, it looked like he would have a long and promising stay at LSU until he graduated. But once again, it took someone with perceptive eyes to channel Justin's talent in the right direction. Legendary coach, Jerry Sullivan, visited and, after watching for a while, turned and said to the others,

"He will be in the NFL someday," before telling Jutsin's father that they shouldn't wait but should declare their son for the draft after his junior year (Mizutani, 2020).

While all of this helped decide the right direction for the young receiver's future, all the coaches agreed that Justin's time spent watching, tagging along, and practicing with his brothers gave him an extra edge. "It got me to see all those different types of players, all of those big-time players that are making noise in the league, and seeing all that, it got me more educated than a lot of young players" (Mizutani, 2020).

A Rising Star

Having all this information and watching him play, made it easy for the Minnesota Vikings to select him in the first round of the 2020 Draft. He went on to set a record of 1,400 receiving yards by a rookie. He bettered that year by year, ending 2022 with his best figures to date. Not only that, but he also pulled some of the most amazing catches that earned him Offensive Player of the Year.

Toward the end of 2023, Justin was on a continued upswing in his career as he became the fastest player in the NFL to score 5,000 yards, doing it in just 52 games (Nettuno, 2023). His ingenuity and speed are a deadly combination that continues to impact every game, and the best part is, he's only in the beginning days of his career. There is so much more to come.

With talented stars like Justin Jefferson, the modern version of the NFL has become a breathtaking, exciting sport to watch and follow.

Helpful Handoffs

Justin knows the importance of support, and you can too if you make sure you have these locked in:

- **Family and friends:** These are the important people in your life. Love and respect them because they will help you to get where you are going.

- **Honor others:** Learn to praise other people for who they are and what they do. Only then, will they truly begin to do the same for you.

- **Learn from people:** Everyone has something to teach you—everyone! Don't think you know it all or that others can't help.

Chapter 14:

Jerry Rice (World)

Career Highlights

- Super Bowl champion: 3
- First Team All-Pro: 10
- Most career receptions: 1,549

- Super Bowl MVP: 1
- Pro Bowl: 13
- Most career touchdowns: 208

(*Jerry Rice*, n.d.)

Perseverance

Pushing through and carrying on is what sets champions apart from one-hit wonders. Persevering when everything is against you or seems like a waste of time can be really tough, but it's something that great people learn, and it's what carries them past the slump, the dry times, and onto the next win.

Jerry Rice learned from a young age that hard work pays off. He learned that real fame and glory only come through blood, sweat, and tears. Otherwise, it vanishes quickly, and you're a nobody. It's about putting in the hours and carrying on when everyone else wants to give up. That's what makes you great. As Jerry himself said, "Today I will do what others won't, so tomorrow I can accomplish what others can't" (Powell, 2016).

Not Into Football

Jerry was one of eight children. Born in 1962 in Starkville, Mississippi, he was not from a wealthy family, and often, there was only just enough food on the table and not enough clothes for more than a couple of outfits. As a bricklayer, Jerry's father worked long hours and was a tough man to please. His way of teaching his kids was to take them along to sites and have them work alongside him. Those long, hot summers passing bricks were not fun, but they ingrained in Jerry the value of hard work.

Jerry knew nothing about football because his mother wouldn't let him play! He had no desire to play the sport anyway. What he did know was how to run, and he would race up and down the dusty road near his house. As a student, Jerry was not very good and struggled with his grades all through high school. One day, as he was sneaking out of yet another class, the vice principal saw him and gave chase. Jerry sprinted his hardest but was eventually caught. The vice principal decided to punish him by putting his talent to good use and sent him across to the football coach.

After a few tryouts, he was slotted in as a wide receiver and began to attract attention. College scouts crowded in to get the quick, nimble runner into their squads. But Jerry rejected all the major colleges and chose the humble Mississippi Valley State University because they were the only ones who personally visited him (Marvi, 2022).

A Decent Start

MVSU was the best platform for Jerry. Under the unorthodox coaching methods of Archie Cooley, he was forced to hone his skills, becoming better and better each year. In 1983, he posted new NCAA single-season records with 102 receptions and 1,450 receiving yards with 14 touchdowns (Marvi, 2022). The next year was even better, breaking his previous performances. Not only did he pick up the nickname "World" because he could catch any ball anywhere in the world, but he was named MVP.

This was enough for him to be noticed, and the San Francisco 49ers grabbed him in the NFL Draft. His first season was not great, as he struggled to get the plays right. It was only later that he realized he was trying so hard to memorize and think through every step instead of relying on his instinctive talent. He ended up with 927 yards and the Rookie of the Year award.

Breaking Through

In 1986, he put on 1,570 yards and 15 touchdowns, and then in 1987 scored 1,078 yards and a new record of 22 receiving touchdowns (Marvi, 2022). More awards rolled in for the young wideout. The team struggled in 1988, even though Rice continued his incredible catching and running, and it was only by winning their last four games that they made it into the playoffs.

They stormed through and found themselves in Super Bowl XXIII. Against the Cincinnati Bengals, the game was held up at 3–3 at halftime until the last quarter saw the game slip away from the 49ers. Calm under pressure, Joe Montana and Jerry Rice worked their magic to pull off an incredible comeback and win. Jerry was Super Bowl MVP with 215 yards on 11 catches (Marvi, 2022).

If that was sensational, then 1989 would go down as extraordinary! The 49ers bullied their way through to the playoffs, where they slaughtered the opposition. The Super Bowl that year was a one-sided affair, with Jerry cashing in 148 yards and three touchdowns to help his team to a 55–10 victory over the Broncos (Marvi, 2022). The outfit from San Francisco was unstoppable.

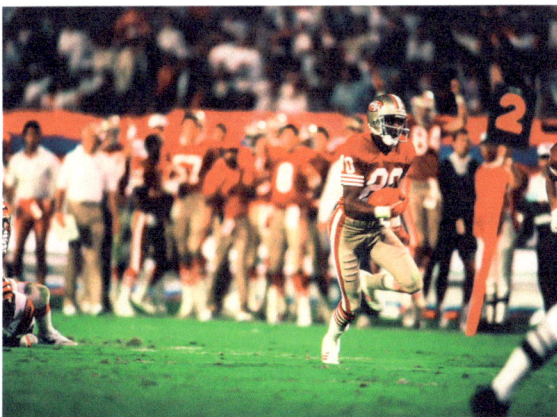

The early '90s saw a few changes, and although Jerry raced on to add to his impressive stats, the team as a whole couldn't get over the finish line. It wasn't until 1994, with a new quarterback, that they were able to get their hands on the Super Bowl trophy again. The following years saw the team battle it out and get close, but it was not enough. Jerry, despite getting older, racked up his best scores of 122 receptions in 1996, leading to 1,848 receiving yards (Marvi, 2022).

Jerry moved over to the Raiders and then the Seahawks, where he played out the rest of his career until retiring after 20 seasons. He held 36 records and scored the most touchdowns in NFL history.

Putting in the Yards

Jerry's secret was not being good at something, but looking to be the best at what he did. This only came through hard work, something he had learned from his father. He never stopped training, even between seasons, and could often be found sprinting in Edgewood County Park and Natural Preserve to tackle the steepest hills. When asked about the training, Jerry answered, "We did this, and it's what made us capable of outdoing everybody else during the football season. It was about being able to put your body through pain" (Marvi, 2022).

If that wasn't enough, he went to speech lessons so he could respond better in media press conferences. Jerry was always looking for ways to become better, and he knew that the only way was to put in the extra yards! It's why he is one of the greatest NFL legends the game has ever seen.

Helpful Handoffs

Jerry's career can teach you a few things that can really help you find what you're good at and persevere with it:

- **Try new things:** Even if you're not sure what you are good at or what you really enjoy, you can find it by doing things you've never tried out before.

- **Be open to ideas:** Don't ignore other sports, hobbies, or interests just because you don't like them. Listen, watch, and learn what you can.

- **Commit yourself:** Hopping from one thing to the next is never good. Stick with something for a while until you're sure you've done your best before moving on.

Chapter 15:

Peculiar and Puzzling Plays

The game of sports has exhilarating, nail-biting moments that get a crowd screaming. But there are also some incidents that are just downright funny. Things that don't quite work out the way they should, leaving everyone in hysterics (especially when you get to watch them on video over and over again!).

Butt Fumble

Mark Sanchez of the New York Jets tried to make a quick play against the Patriots in a game. He took the snap in broken play and decided to roll to the right to create a chance to make something happen. Instead, he slipped and charged straight into the backside of one of his own linemen. It was such a hard knock that Sanchez dropped the ball, and the Patriots swooped down to pick it up and score a touchdown.

Fail Mary

At the end of 2012, referees were on strike. So, replacements were brought in, although they were not as good as the proper officials. Toward the end of a Packers and Seahawks game, a Hail Mary pass was thrown and was fought for by both teams. Before they could talk it through among themselves, the refs each signaled their call. One showed it as a touchdown, while the other signaled an interception. It was chaos until a Seahawks' touchdown was eventually awarded.

Own Tackle

Confusion out in the middle happens. There are so many plays to remember and people running everywhere. But as professional sportsmen, they're expected (and paid) to figure it out and react smoothly and calmly. It's not always the case, and Ray-Ray Armstrong dropping his own teammate with a heavy tackle on a punt return just goes to show that they're also human.

Celebrations

There was a time when the referees came down hard on these silly antics that happened after a touchdown or a game-win. But they've relaxed a bit, and the crazy performances continue. Terrel Owens will be remembered for grabbing pom-poms and doing a victory dance, as will Chad Johnson for his Tiger Woods putting impersonations and making himself a H.O.F. (Hall of Fame) jacket. A backflip, a high five, or the usual dance of joy all bring delight to the fans.

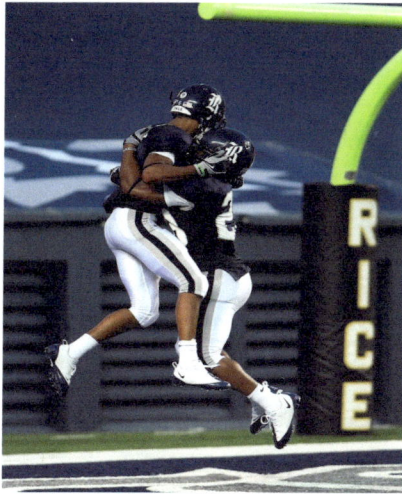

The Wrong Way

Vikings player Jim Marshall picked up the ball and started sprinting to victory. It was too easy. No one was tackling him, and there were no blocks in his path. Arriving in the end zone when the crowd is not cheering and your opposing team is clapping for you must tell you something is wrong. Marshall had run the wrong way, to the 49ers side. They even congratulated him afterward. To make it even sweeter, Roy Riegels, who did the same thing back in the 1929 Rose Bowl, wrote Marshall a letter that said, "Welcome to the club" (Tull, n.d.).

Helmet Catch

One of the strangest and most awesome catches was in Super Bowl XLII between the Patriots and Giants. New England was up, looking to close out a perfect season on 18–0, but it wasn't going to be. Not with Giant's David Tyree on the field! In the last few minutes, a high 32-yard throw from the quarterback saw Tyree leap off the ground and get one hand onto the ball. Pressing it against his helmet, he held onto the ball as he fell down to gain advantage. They scored soon after to close the game out with a loss but denied the Patriots their clean sheet! (Reardon, 2022).

Double Doink

For the Chicago Bears in the NFC playoffs, 2018 was a heartbreaking moment. With the Eagles leading 16–15, the Chicago quarterback got his team down the field to be just within reach of a goal attempt. With 10 seconds on the clock, all Cody Parker had to do was slot the ball between the posts and win. He lined up and kicked. It cleared the 43 yards easily but connected with one player on the way before hitting the upright post and bouncing down onto the crossbar back into the end zone (Reardon, 2022). They lost by one point, denied by the poles!

Chapter 16:

Tristan Wirfs

Career Highlights (So Far)

- Super Bowl champion: 1
- Pro Bowl: 2
- First Team All-Pro: 1

(*Tristan Wirfs*, n.d.)

Dealing With Pressure

The pressures of professional sports can get to a player. The expectation to perform every game, the constant media, and the traveling, can all become a bit too much. It's not easy to keep your headspace when you're dealing with all these demands. And on top of that, you have to deal with your own personal issues. Too often, players choose other ways to drown out the noise of it all, but it can still become a burden if it's not dealt with.

In Tristan Wirfs' case, he chose a healthier route. His position in football was suddenly made more difficult, and he struggled to adapt. His mind was going crazy. Instead of collapsing, he opted for a healthier option, which may have seemed weak many years ago but today is helping many players like him to adapt.

A Mom's Sacrifice

Tristan loves his mother. He gives her a hug before every game, and he's not embarrassed about it. Sarah is one of the reasons he is wearing a Tampa Bay Buccaneers uniform. His father is not in the picture, and Tristan's family had to live in a trailer-park home until they could finally find a house in Mount

Vernon. His grandmother looked after him and his sister while Sarah worked shifts to provide for them. With no father, Tristan played catch with a fence in the backyard.

In high school, Tristan showed he had real athletic abilities. Not only did he play football, but he starred as a wrestler, winning a state title when he shed 30 pounds as his commitment to the sport. He also did well in discus and shot put, but it was in football that he really shone, resulting in a scholarship to Iowa State in 2017. After his time at college, he headed out to the NFL, where he was drafted into Tampa Bay.

He admits that it would not have happened if it had not been for all his mother's late-night shifts. He also points out Coach Ferentz from Iowa State, who prepared him for the big leap into professional sports. He says:

> Playing at Iowa was a big part of turning me into who I am today. Coach Ferentz runs his program at Iowa like a professional team. He does his best to turn us into better men, good husbands, good fathers, and good people in the community. My mom was also a huge part of that, but Coach Ferentz continued that at Iowa. (Frotscher, n.d., para. 9)

A Promising Start

Tristan is big. He towers over the opposition. Add in his weight and he is a force to be reckoned with. Training with weights, he has built himself up into a wall of muscle. Starting all 20 games, he blocked for the legendary Tom Brady (allowing only one sack) and was part of a winning team that reached the Super Bowl in 2020, winning it against the Kansas City Chiefs 31–9 (Frotscher, n.d.).

His next season was interrupted by injury, but he was still named to the Pro Bowl and All-Pro selection. In 2021, there was a similar outcome with the young tackler getting better and better at what he does. Brady had only positives about him:

> He's really learning how to be a real professional, and he takes his job seriously. He's obviously talented; just his size (6-foot-5, 320 pounds), his ability to keep people out of the backfield. Very difficult to go through and he's very hard to go around. He doesn't get beat very often—very, very, very rarely. (Knight, 2022, para. 15)

Tristan was named Pro Bowl again in 2022, his second in only three years. For the big man, making blocks and tackles is winning him recognition and fame.

Mentally Strong

But it wasn't all that easy. Tristan was plagued with self-doubt since stepping into his Tampa Bay outfit. He questioned whether he was good enough, especially to play next to Tom Brady. The negative thinking got worse when his coach decided to switch him from right tackle to left. Tristan tried but really found it got to him, and he could not adapt properly. Instead of hiding his mental struggles, he has been open about it, going to see a psychologist.

Rather than act brave around his teammates, he made a stand to address his issues. He said:

> It seems like so minuscule, like, "Oh, you're just flipping sides," but I was like having breakdowns about it. I'm like, "I can't sit here with these thoughts anymore, I'm just kind of setting myself up for failure." I would just think about, "I am going to suck" or like, "I am not going to be able to do it" all day long. (Scott, 2023, para. 5)

It's a bold move that is beginning to pay off. His confidence has increased, and his coaches are behind him every step of the way. And Tristan's not about to step back any time soon. "They trust me and they put me in this position. I want to go out there and do the best that I can and show that I can do it" (Scott, 2023).

Helpful Handoffs

Dealing with pressure is tough, but just like Tristan did, there are ways that can help in those tough times:

- **Recognize your emotions:** We all get angry, happy, disappointed. It helps to know when and why you are feeling this way so you can control the way you react.

- **People you can talk to:** Keeping everything bottled up leads to bad reactions. Talking about your feelings is the best way to deal with them.

- **Find coping strategies:** There are ways to not let your emotions get the better of you. Learning how to breathe, count slowly, or calm yourself in certain moments will be good as you grow up.

Conclusion

It would be great if heroes were born that way, like Superman was. His super strength and planet-saving abilities were with him as a baby on Krypton. But the real world is not a comic book or a movie. Heroes are never born; they are made. They might have some incredible skills that make them extra fast, amazingly clever, or exceptionally powerful. But with all those gifts, a person can just as easily become a villain or a fallen hero.

The world of sports is filled with great athletes who are not that good at being upstanding role models. Having the best throwing arm doesn't make you the world's favorite quarterback. Having the biggest chest doesn't make you the most loved offensive player. That is all up to character!

Players who learn to overcome adversity, stand on their own two feet despite setbacks, and honor the people who lead and guide them are the ones who shine. These are the ones that stand tall at the end of a game, not just because they have won, but because they have their integrity.

This book lists only a few players who are rated for both their skill on the field and their faith and perseverance off the field.

Tom Brady, Jerry Rice, Tom Dempsey, and Patrick Mahomes had to earn their spot on the team. They had to push through, dig deep, and make their mark by gritting their teeth, believing, and reaching for their goals.

These players may not be 100% squeaky clean. They have moments of anger, weakness, and disappointment because they aren't Superman. They are human, just like everyone else. Putting them up as role models or heroes doesn't mean they won't fall or fail—it just means they have learned how to get up when they're knocked down.

That's what sets them apart.

Life threw curveballs at each of the players listed in this book. Some were benched in the middle of games, others were injured, and many were overlooked. But each one found faith. It may have been in God. It may have been in the dreams they set for themselves. It may have been instilled in them by their parents. Belief is what sets them up to overcome the hurdles. They rose above the normal pitfalls of life to become bright stars in a game that is loved by so many across the country.

Their posters are stuck on walls, cards with their pictures are traded, and screensavers with their faces flash on phones and computers. Shirts are worn with the numbers of these players, to show that they are admired. Jalen Hurts smiles at you from your TV, reminding you that if he can do it, then maybe you can too. Kurt Warner kept on pushing to show that anything is possible.

It's not about football (although it's a pretty cool game). It's about far more than that. It's about your life, your goals, your attitude, your character, your faith. Taking lessons from these great players can help you to succeed in different areas. You can also overcome, rise up, and dominate the field of life.

References

admin. (2022, July 19). *Walter Payton—"Never die easy. Why run out of bounds and die easy?"* eWritingCafe. https://ewritingcafe.com/walter-payton-never-die-easy-why-run-out-of-bounds-and-die-easy-make-that-l/#google_vignette

Alonso, D. (2023, February 12). *Jalen Hurts' story: From being humiliated to playing in the Super Bowl.* MARCA. https://www.marca.com/en/nfl/philadelphia-eagles/2023/02/12/63e8b5a4268e3e9e728b4576.html

Barrera, D. (2019, September 8). *6 of the strangest rules in the NFL.* Sportscasting | Pure Sports. https://www.sportscasting.com/6-of-the-strangest-rules-in-the-nfl/

Bearn, J. (2007). *Reggie White.* Pennsylvania Center for the Book. https://pabook.libraries.psu.edu/literary-cultural-heritage-map-pa/bios/White__Reggie

Bradley, J. E. (1993, November 15). *Like father, like son: Peyton and Archie Manning.* Sports Illustrated Vault. https://vault.si.com/vault/1993/11/15/like-father-like-son-ole-miss-will-never-forget-archie-but-peyton-is-the-manning-of-the-year-with-recruiters-from-oxford-to-ann-arbor

Brobeck, G. (2016, March 7). *Peyton Manning's career and legacy.* WATE 6 on Your Side. https://www.wate.com/news/peyton-mannings-career-and-legacy/

Conn, J. R. (2023, February 10). *A phenom's résumé and an underdog's story: The journey of Jalen Hurts.* The Ringer. https://www.theringer.com/nfl/2023/2/10/23593257/jalen-hurts-super-bowl-philadelphia-eagles-alabama-oklahoma

Cronin, C. (2020, May 15). *How Justin Jefferson went from zero-star recruit to Vikings' first-round pick.* ESPN.com. https://www.espn.com/blog/minnesota-vikings/post/_/id/29921/how-justin-jefferson-went-from-zero-star-recruit-to-vikings-first-round-pick

Dallas, K. (2023, February 7). *This year's Super Bowl features two quarterbacks who talk openly about faith.* Deseret News. https://www.deseret.com/faith/2023/2/7/23589206/patrick-mahomes-religion-jalen-hurts

Deen, S. (2023, February 1). *Tom Brady's stats, records—and the teams he loved and hated to face as he retires from NFL.* USA TODAY. https://www.usatoday.com/story/sports/nfl/2023/02/01/tom-brady-stats-records-nfl-retirement/11162812002/

Donahue, B. (2022, April 15). *The life and career of Walter Payton (complete story).* Pro Football History. https://www.profootballhistory.com/walter-payton/

Donahue, B. (2023, August 20). *The life and career of Tom Dempsey (story).* Pro Football History. https://www.profootballhistory.com/tom-dempsey/

Epstein, J. (2022, January 24). *"Be the Grim Reaper": How Chiefs, Patrick Mahomes outlasted Bills, Josh Allen in battle of QB excellence.* USA TODAY. https://www.usatoday.com/story/sports/nfl/chiefs/2022/01/24/patrick-mahomes-grim-reaper-kansas-city-chiefs-buffalo-bills/6633507001/

Faith on the Field. (2021, October 6). *Jalen Hurts credits his direction in life to God and his dad.* Faith on the Field. https://faithonthefieldshow.com/jalen-hurts-credits-his-direction-in-life-to-god-and-his-dad/

Foust, M. (2021, December 30). *Kurt Warner reveals moment he realized God is not a "spare tire"—I had it mixed up.* ChristianHeadlines. https://www.christianheadlines.com/contributors/michael-foust/kurt-warner-reveals-moment-he-realized-god-is-not-a-spare-tire-i-had-it-mixed-up.html

Freedman, A. (2023, February 9). *All the rules you probably didn't know NFL players have to follow*. Men's Health. https://www.menshealth.com/entertainment/g35005358/rules-nfl-players-follow/

Frotscher, B. (n.d.). *Tristan Wirfs reflects on a super rookie season*. Iowa Center for Advancement. https://www.foriowa.org/iowa-stories/iowa-story.php?namer=true&isid=122

Gagnon, B. (2016, March 6). *"Whatever he says, you gotta do": Teammates remember the Peyton Manning way*. Bleacher Report. https://bleacherreport.com/articles/2619431-whatever-he-says-you-gotta-do-teammates-remember-the-peyton-manning-way

Gaines, C. (2023, February 1). *Why Tom Brady was overlooked in the NFL Draft and why it was more than luck that led him to the Patriots*. Business Insider. https://www.businessinsider.com/new-england-patriots-draft-tom-brady-sixth-round-pick-2022-2

Goldstein, R. (2020, April 5). Tom Dempsey, record-setting kicker, dies at 73. *The New York Times*. https://www.nytimes.com/2020/04/05/obituaries/tom-dempsey-dead.html

Hunt, D. J. (2023, October 4). *Kurt Warner: Career retrospective*. Yardbarker. https://www.yardbarker.com/nfl/articles/kurt_warner_career_retrospective_100423/s1__38062976#slide_1

Jalen Hurts—Philadelphia Eagles quarterback. (n.d.). StatMuse. Retrieved November 25, 2023, from https://www.statmuse.com/nfl/player/jalen-hurts-28205

Jerry Rice—San Francisco 49ers wide receiver. (n.d.). StatMuse. Retrieved November 25, 2023, from https://www.statmuse.com/nfl/player/jerry-rice-17187

Justin Jefferson overview. (n.d.). StatMuse. Retrieved November 25, 2023, from https://www.statmuse.com/nfl/player/justin-jefferson-28163

Knight, J. (2022, December 23). *It's early, but Bucs Pro Bowler Tristan Wirfs is putting together Canton credentials.* Tampa Bay Times. https://www.tampabay.com/sports/bucs/2022/12/22/bucs-tristan-wirfs-pro-bowl-tom-brady-ladainian-tomlinson/

Kurt Warner—Arizona Cardinals quarterback. (n.d.). StatMuse. Retrieved November 25, 2023, from https://www.statmuse.com/nfl/player/kurt-warner-21572

Lopez, S. (2023, January 31). *10 things to know about Patrick Mahomes: Two-time Super Bowl MVP, champion.* Dallas News. https://www.dallasnews.com/sports/texas-tech-red-raiders/2023/02/12/10-things-to-know-about-patrick-mahomes-two-time-super-bowl-mvp-champion/

Machota, J. (2023, August 21). *NFL stadium rankings: All 30 NFL venues from best to worst.* The Athletic. https://theathletic.com/4783340/2023/08/21/nfl-stadium-rankings-all-30-nfl-venues-from-best-to-worst/

Marie, J. (2013, June 12). *The most insane coaches in sports.* Bleacher Report. https://bleacherreport.com/articles/1699856-the-most-insane-coaches-in-sports

Marinelli, D. (2022, November 12). *Packers: A look back at the legendary Reggie White.* Lombardi Ave. https://lombardiave.com/2022/11/12/packers-legendary-reggie-white/

Marvi, R. (2022, February 7). *The life and career of Jerry Rice (complete story).* Pro Football History. https://www.profootballhistory.com/jerry-rice/

Mizutani, D. (2020, September 25). *Vikings rookie Justin Jefferson still writing his story.* Twin Cities. https://www.twincities.com/2020/09/25/all-in-the-family-vikings-rookie-justin-jefferson-still-writing-his-story/

Morales, O. (2009, February 3). *Kurt Warner: The story of a warrior.* Bleacher Report. https://bleacherreport.com/articles/119048-kurt-warner-the-story-of-a-warrior

Morthier, M. C. (2022, September 20). *Inspiring story of Tom "The Bomb" Dempsey.* The Sports Column. https://www.thesportscol.com/2022/09/inspiring-story-of-tom-the-bomb-dempsey/

Munez, E. (2023, October 25). *Jalen Hurts | quarterback, Philadelphia Eagles, biography, & facts.* Britannica. https://www.britannica.com/biography/Jalen-Hurts

Nettuno, T. (2023, September 15). *Justin Jefferson makes history with huge performance in Thursday Night Football.* Yahoo Sports. https://sports.yahoo.com/justin-jefferson-makes-history-huge-184026007.html

Passalacqua, F. (2011, July 9). *12 strangest injuries in NFL history.* Bleacher Report. https://bleacherreport.com/articles/762058-top-12-stangest-injuries-in-nfl-history

Patrick Mahomes overview. (n.d.). StatMuse. Retrieved November 25, 2023, from https://www.statmuse.com/nfl/player/patrick-mahomes-25894

Peyton Manning—Indianapolis Colts Quarterback. (n.d.). StatMuse. Retrieved November 25, 2023, from https://www.statmuse.com/nfl/player/peyton-manning-12935

Powell, B. (2016, November 21). *What are you doing to be great? (#1).* 100 Naked Words. https://medium.com/100-naked-words/what-are-you-doing-to-be-great-1-9df1e4ea29c5

Reardon, L. (2022, December 19). *Ranking the most infamous and wild plays in NFL history.* NBC Sports Boston. https://www.nbcsportsboston.com/nfl/new-england-patriots/ranking-the-most-infamous-and-wild-plays-in-nfl-history/279705/

Reggie White–Philadelphia Eagles defensive lineman. (n.d.). StatMuse. Retrieved November 25, 2023, from https://www.statmuse.com/nfl/player/reggie-white-22087

Robinson, S. (2023, September 13). *NFL players who returned from devastating injuries.* Yardbarker. https://www.yardbarker.com/nfl/articles/nfl_players_who_returned_from_devastating_injuries_091323/s1__33229937#slide_23

Rollins, K. (2020, January 19). *What coach has the most Super Bowl wins?* Sports Illustrated. https://www.si.com/nfl/2019/02/03/coach-most-super-bowl-wins-all-time-record-history

Schoenbeck, D. (2023, February 2). *Famous hard work beats talent quotes.* Dave Schoenbeck. https://daveschoenbeck.com/hard-work-beats-talent-quotes/

Scott, J. (2023, August 4). *Buccaneers' All-Pro shares why a position change led him to seeing a psychologist.* Sports Illustrated. https://www.si.com/nfl/2023/08/04/buccaneers-all-pro-tristan-wirfs-shares-why-position-change-led-to-seeing-psychologist

Seaver, C. (2022, August 6). *The history of American football and its growth as a game.* History Defined. https://www.historydefined.net/history-of-american-football/

Straeter, K. (2023, February 4). *Peyton Manning shares the shocking reason why he loves Jesus, drinks beer, & won't pray to win.* Faithit. https://faithit.com/peyton-manning-shares-the-shocking-reason-why-he-loves-jesus-drinks-beer-wont-pray-to-win-entertainment/

Tom Brady overview. (n.d.). StatMuse. https://www.statmuse.com/nfl/player/tom-brady-2054

Tom Dempsey—Philadelphia Eagles kicker. (n.d.). StatMuse. Retrieved November 25, 2023, from https://www.statmuse.com/nfl/player/tom-dempsey-5090

Tristan Wirfs—Tampa Bay Buccaneers offensive lineman. (n.d.). StatMuse. Retrieved November 25, 2023, from https://www.statmuse.com/nfl/player/tristan-wirfs-28167

Tull, P. (n.d.). *Top 10 funniest NFL fails.* WatchMojo. Retrieved November 8, 2023, from https://www.watchmojo.com/articles/top-10-funniest-nfl-fails

Walter Payton—Chicago Bears running back. (n.d.). StatMuse. Retrieved November 25, 2023, from https://www.statmuse.com/nfl/player/walter-payton-16001

Image References

12019. (2103, March 6). *Landover, Maryland, FedEx field image* [Image]. Pixabay. https://pixabay.com/photos/landover-maryland-fedex-field-89813/

All-Pro Reels. (2013, January 4). *Kirk Cousins* [Image]. Wikipedia. https://en.wikipedia.org/wiki/File:Kirk_Cousins.jpg

All-Pro-Reels. (2021, January 9). *Tristan Wirfs* [Image]. Wikimedia Commons. https://upload.wikimedia.org/wikipedia/commons/e/ea/Tristan_Wirfs_%2850832403298%29_%28croppe

All-Pro Reels. (2021, October 17). *Patrick Mahomes on the run* [Image]. Wikimedia Commons. https://commons.wikimedia.org/wiki/File:Patrick_Mahomes_on_the_run_%2851616124184%29.jpg

All-Pro Reels. (2022, September 25). *Jalen Hurts 2022 Eagles* [Image]. Wikimedia Commons. https://upload.wikimedia.org/wikipedia/commons/c/c6/Jalen_Hurts_2022_Eagles_%28cropped%29.jpg

Andy Henderson. (2021, January 15). *The toss* [Image]. Unsplash. https://unsplash.com/photos/group-of-people-in-white-and-black-shirts-mRoISP4jcnA

August Schwerdfeger. (2021, September 23). *U.S. Bank Stadium 2021-09-23* [Image]. Wikimedia Commons. https://upload.wikimedia.org/wikipedia/commons/c/c5/U.S._Bank_Stadium_2021-09-23.jpg

BrokenSphere. (2008, December 14). *Oakland Coliseum field from Mt. Davis* [Image]. Wikimedia Commons. https://upload.wikimedia.org/wikipedia/commons/b/b6/Oakland_Coliseum_field_from_Mt._Davis.JPG

Charli Christ. (2021, July 20). *Tom Brady* [Image]. Wikimedia Commons. https://commons.wikimedia.org/wiki/File:Tom_Brady_2021.png

Cian Leach. (2020, October 29). *Football players in red and white jersey shirt and black shorts* [Image]. Unsplash. https://unsplash.com/photos/football-players-in-red-and-white-jersey-shirt-and-black-shorts-2vb858vvkys

Darb02. (2016, July 24). *US Bank Stadium interior—Minnesota Vikings orientation* [Image]. Wikimedia Commons. https://upload.wikimedia.org/wikipedia/commons/7/70/US_Bank_Stadium_interior_-_Minnesota_Vikings_orientation.jpg

Dick Sorda. (1975). *Tom Dempsey 1975* [Image]. Wikimedia Commons. https://upload.wikimedia.org/wikipedia/commons/3/3b/Tom_Dempsey_1975.jpg

Don Bray. (2007, February 10). *Peyton Manning passes at 2007 Pro Bowl* [Image]. Wikimedia Commons. https://upload.wikimedia.org/wikipedia/commons/5/56/Peyton_Manning_passes_at_2007_Pro_Bowl_070210-N-9076B-049.jpg

Etsy. (2023, December 1). *Digital Poster of Reggie White Poster* [Image]. Etsy. https://www.etsy.com/listing/1579822004/digital-poster-of-reggie-white-poster?ga_order=most_relevant&ga_search_type=all&ga_view_ty

pe=gallery&ga_search_query=reggie+white&ref=sr_gallery-1-
1&sts=1&dd=1&organic_search_click=1

football wife. (2018, November 20). *Man in blue and white jacket wearing black helmet* [Image]. Pexels. https://www.pexels.com/photo/man-in-blue-and-white-jacket-wearing-black-helmet-1618044/

Jack Newton. (2008, November 11). *Kevin Faulk and Marcus Buggs* [Image]. Wikimedia Commons. https://upload.wikimedia.org/wikipedia/commons/d/dd/Kevin_Faulk _and_Marcus_Buggs.jpg

Jeno's. (1984, October 7). *1986 Jeno's Pizza - #12 Walter Payton* [Image]. Wikimedia Commons. https://commons.wikimedia.org/wiki/File:1986_Jeno%27s_Pizza_- _12_-_Walter_Payton.jpg

Jerry Coli. (n.d.) *Jerry Rice* [Image]. Dreamstime. https://www.dreamstime.com/royalty-free-stock-image-jerry-rice-image27968306

Jerry Coli. (n.d.) *San Francisco 49ers WR Jerry Rice* [Image]. Dreamstime. https://www.dreamstime.com/editorial-stock-image-jerry-rice-san-francisco-ers-wr-image-taken-color-slide-image73823924

Jerry Coli. (n.d.) *Kurt Warner* [Image]. Dreamstime. https://www.dreamstime.com/royalty-free-stock-image-kurt-warner-former-st-louis-rams-qb-image-taken-color-slide-image36807046

Jerry Coli. (n.d.) *Peyton Manning* [Image]. Dreamstime. https://www.dreamstime.com/editorial-stock-image-peyton-manning-colts-qb-image-taken-color-slide-image76343729

Jerry Coli. (n.d.) *Peyton Manning Indianapolis Colts* [Image]. Dreamstime. https://www.dreamstime.com/royalty-free-stock-image-peyton-manning-indianapolis-colts-image17877696

KeithJJ. (2016, June 9). *Football, American football* [Image]. Pixabay. https://pixabay.com/photos/football-american-football-1445079/

Lance Cpl. Edward L. Mennenga, USMC. (2005, February 6). *Patriots on offense at Super Bowl XXXIX* [Image]. Wikimedia Commons. https://commons.wikimedia.org/wiki/File:Patriots_on_offense_at_S uper_Bowl_XXXIX_1.jpg

LSUvsUT 292. (2019, October 5). *LSUvsUT 292* [Image]. Wikimedia Commons. https://upload.wikimedia.org/wikipedia/commons/3/38/LSUvsUT_2 92_%2849175057142%29.jpg

Mahomes family. (2023, February 2). *Patrick Mahomes with his father Pat Mahomes in his childhood days* [Image]. New York Post. https://nypost.com/2023/02/02/patrick-mahomes-father-knew-he-was-a-natural-athlete-from-youth-days-in-mets-infield/

Moses8910. (2020, June 26). *The Soldier Field* [Image]. Wikimedia Commons. https://upload.wikimedia.org/wikipedia/commons/e/ee/The_Soldier _Field.jpg

Own Work. (2013, July 27). *Austrian Bowl 2013-103* [Image]. Wikimedia Commons. https://upload.wikimedia.org/wikipedia/commons/4/45/Austrian_Bo wl_2013-103.JPG

Pixabay. (2005, December 3). *8 football Referees in the field* [Image]. Pexels. https://www.pexels.com/photo/8-football-referees-in-the-field-163435/

Pixabay. (2008, November 8). *Clashing football players* [Image]. Pexels. https://www.pexels.com/photo/clashing-football-players-264300/

Peter Griffin. (n.d.). *Posterization of Peyton Manning* [Image]. PublicDomainPictues.net. https://www.publicdomainpictures.net/en/view-image.php?image=230614&picture=posterization-of-peyton-manning

Peter Griffin. (n.d.). *Posterization of Walter Payton* [Image]. PublicDomainPictues.net.

https://www.publicdomainpictures.net/en/view-image.php?image=230488&picture=posterization-of-walter-payton

Smart Destinations. (2005, April 28). *Qwest Field North* [Image]. Wikimedia Commons. https://upload.wikimedia.org/wikipedia/commons/5/53/Qwest_Field_North.jpg

Wikipedia. (2023, October 11). *Walter Camp* [Image]. Wikipedia. https://en.wikipedia.org/wiki/Walter_Camp#/media/File:Walter_Camp_-_Project_Gutenberg_eText_18048.jpg

Made in United States
Troutdale, OR
03/07/2025